WITHDRAWN

Wedded Bliss

A Victorian Bride's Handbook

To:

_____

_____

From:

_____

_____

Molly Dolan Blayney

Wedded Bliss

A Victorian Bride's
❧ Handbook ❧

Collages by Molly Dolan Blayney

Photographed by Monica Stevenson

Abbeville Press ♥ Publishers

New York ♥ London ♥ Paris

Contents

MANY VOLUMES OF GOOD WISHES

Here's volumes of Good Wishes,
And so many I've in store
For you, dear Friend
That I could send,
You twice as many more.

MY
OWN
DEAR
LOVE.

An
Introduction
to Love

First Blush

You have seen Miss Dalton! You have met her in all the elegance of ball costume; your eye has feasted on her elegant figure, and upon her eye sparkling with the consciousness of beauty. You have talked with Miss Dalton about Byron,—about Wordsworth,—about Homer. You have quoted poetry to Miss Dalton; you have clasped Miss Dalton's hand!

Her conversation delights you by its piquancy and grace; she is quite ready to meet you (a grave matter of surprise!) upon whatever subject you may suggest. You lapse easily and lovingly into the current of her thought, and blush to find yourself vacantly admiring, when she is looking for reply. The regard you feel for her, resolves itself into an exquisite mental love, vastly superior as you think, to any other kind of love. There is no dream of marriage as yet, but only of sitting beside her in the moonlight, during a countless succession of hours, and talking of poetry and nature,—of destiny, and love.

Magnificent Miss Dalton!

Donald G. Mitchell
Dream Life, 1851

On the Street

It is the privilege of the lady to determine whether she will recognize a gentleman after an introduction, and he is bound to return the bow. In bowing to a lady on the street, it is not enough that a gentleman should touch his hat, he should lift it from his head. . . .

A bow should never be accompanied by a broad smile, even when you are well acquainted, . . . and yet you should never speak to an acquaintance without a smile in your eyes.

John H. Young
Our Deportment, 1881

Love's Telegraph

If a gentleman want a wife, he wears a ring on the *first* finger of the left hand; if he be engaged, he wears it on the *second* finger; if married, on the *third*; and on the fourth if he never intends to be married. When a lady is not engaged, she wears a hoop or diamond on her first finger; if engaged, on the second; if married, on the third; and on the fourth if she intends to die unmarried. When a gentleman presents a fan, flower, or trinket, to a lady with the *left* hand, this, on his part, is an overture of regard; should she receive it with the *left* hand, it is considered as an acceptance of his esteem; but if with the *right* hand, it is a refusal of the offer. Thus, by a few simple tokens explained by rule, the passion of love is expressed; and through the medium of the telegraph, the most timid and diffident man may, without difficulty, communicate his sentiments of regard to a lady, and, in case his offer should be refused, avoid experiencing the mortification of an explicit refusal.

Anon
Inquire Within, 1895

Advice to Young Women

It is not good form for a young girl to address by his Christian name a man with whom her acquaintance is but slight.

A young girl should consult her mother before granting a request for an interchange of letters with a young man.

Flowers, bonbons, and books are the only gifts that a girl is allowed, as a rule, to accept from a man unless she is engaged to him.

Be merry and pleasant and have a good time, but don't let any man feel that he can treat you with aught but respect.

Don't let him touch the tip of your little finger until he has the right. You'll be glad you didn't when the right man appears.

Fannie Dickerson Chase
Good Form and Social Ethics, 1913

Chaperonage

A chaperon is not to watch and to restrain her, but to certify that her bloom is unimpaired, and to compel others to respect it. No air of cheapness, no breath of slander, no undue familiarity, can touch the girl who is known to be always protected as a thing too precious for the hazard of chance.

William Morse Cole
Chaperonage, 1899

The Ball

A great drawback to balls in America is the lack of convenience for those who wish to remain seated. In Europe, where the elderly are first considered, seats are placed around the room, somewhat high, for the chaperons, and at their feet sit the debutantes. These red-covered sofas, in two tiers, as it were, are brought in by the upholsterer and are very convenient. It is strange that all large halls are not furnished with them, as they make every one comfortable at very little expense, and add to the appearance of the room. A row of well-dressed ladies, in velvet, brocade, and diamonds, some with white hair, certainly forms a very distinguished background for those who sit at their feet.

M. E. W. Sherwood
Manners and Social Usage, 1884

S.D. LAUTER CO.
Sole Agents,

NEWARK, N.J.

E. GABLER & BRO.
NEW YORK.

To her honour
be it remembered,
Queen Victoria has
prohibited the polka
being danced in her
presence.

Eliza Leslie
The Ladies'
Guide, 1864

Remember that the waltz-step
changes every few years, and that
a blunder in dancing is very like a
crime.

Florence Marion Hall
The Correct Thing, 1888

ORONO   JUNE 12.

If you wish to see the fashions and manners of the times, to study men and character, to learn good breeding and politeness without affectation, to see grace and dignity without haughtiness, you will find no place for these observations more proper than the ball-room.

Thomas Hillgrove
Hillgrove's Ball-Room Guide, 1864

If a lady waltz with you, beware not to press her waist; lightly touch it with the open palm of your hand, lest you leave a disagreeable impression.

An American Gentleman
Etiquette for Gentlemen, 1848

GOOD-NIGHT, LADIES!

Sostenuto. For Male Voices. *
f TENORS.

1. Good - night, la - dies! good - night, la - dies!
2. Fare - well, la - dies! fare - well, la - dies!
3. Sweet dreams, la - dies! sweet dreams, la - dies!

f BASSES.

Good - night, la - dies! We're going to leave you now.
Fare - well, la - dies! We're going to leave you now.
Sweet dreams, la - dies! We're going to leave you now.

Allegro.

Mer - ri - ly we roll a - long, roll a - long, roll a - long.

Repeat. pp

Mer - ri - ly we roll a - long, O'er the dark blue sea.

* For mixed voices, ladies should sing tenor parts one octave lower.

No. 2.— Music Post Card Series. (Copyright, 1907,) Tali Esen Morgan,
1947 Broadway, New York City.

How to Stage a Ball

*B*alls are the paradise of daughters, the purgatory of chaperons. . . . The advantage of the ball is that it brings young people together for a sensible and innocent recreation . . . so when Arabella announces that she is engaged to the young and wealthy Sir Thysse Thatte, Bart., it was at one ball he met her, at another he flirted, at a third he courted, and at a fourth offered. . . .

Any number over one hundred constitutes a "large ball," below that number it is simply "a ball," and under fifty "a dance."

In making your list, you must not take in *all* your acquaintance, but only all those who are moveable—the marionettes, in fact. Middle-aged people think it a compliment to be asked to a ball about as much as the boa-constrictor in the Regent's Park would. Both he and they like to be fed, and after five-and-thirty, it is laborious not only to dance, but even to look at dancing.

The requisites for an agreeable ball are good ventilation, good arrangement, a good floor, good music, a good supper, and good company.

In Paris, where balls, in spite of the absence of supper, are more elegant than anywhere else, a vast deal of effect and freshness is secured by the employment of shrubs, plants, and flowers, and these may be freely used without making your rooms fantastic. Thus, that odious entrance from the kitchen stairs, which yawns upon the lobby of most London houses, should be concealed by a thick hedge of rhododendrons in pots; the balustrades of the staircase and gallery should be woven with evergreens, and all the fireplaces should be concealed by plenty of plants in flower.

The best color for a ball-room is very pale yellow. The light should come from the walls, heightened by strong reflectors. A polished floor, whatever the wood, is always the best thing to dance on, and, if you want to give a ball, and not only a crush, you should hire a man who, with a brush under one foot, and a slipper on the other, will dance over the floor for four or five hours, till you can almost see your face in it. Above all, take care that there is not bees'-wax enough to blacken the ladies' shoes. It is the amount of rubbing which must give it the polish.

The dances should be arranged beforehand, and, for large balls you should have printed a number of double cards, containing on the one side a list of the dances; on the other, blank spaces to be filled up by the names of partners. A small pencil should be attached to each card, which should be given to each guest in the cloakroom.

Man in a Club Window
The Habits of Good Society, 1860

*No need had she of borrowed light
To make her beauty fair.*

The Queen's Ball

London, June 16th, 1845
56 Charing Cross

The subject of public interest, which has engrossed everybody's conversation, has been the Queen's dress ball, at which the guests were expected to appear in the costumes of a hundred years ago, and consequently to personate the manners of the court at that time.

At the court ball, it is said, that the dresses of some of the gentlemen, without diamonds, cost five hundred guineas, or more than $2,500, and one lady wore £60,000, or $300,000 worth of diamonds. Lord Morpeth was one of the most elegantly and expensively dressed gentlemen, and seemed himself not a little amused with his wig and appearance. The Duchess of Bedford presided, and was extremely well dressed. The Duchess of Sutherland was most magnificently apparelled, but she is so handsome that nothing appears amiss with her; she wore powder, but no wig. The Duchess of Roxburgh, whom I do not know, appeared most splendidly; and well she might, as the annual income of the Duke is stated to be £300,000.

The dresses of the ladies were without exception extremely modest; more so than I have seen at many evening and dinner parties. The dancing was graceful and elegant, and the old figure dances were pleasing.

The minuet, I hope, will come in fashion again; it is very pleasing and full of grace. But I cannot, under any circumstances, be reconciled to the waltz, which seems to me, except among brothers and sisters, or members of the same family, to border upon indelicacy.

Henry Colman
European Life and Manners, 1849

Calling and → Courting ←

Formula for Telling a Girl's Age

Girls of a marriageable age do not like to tell how old they are; but you can find out by following the subjoined instructions, the young lady doing the figuring: Tell her to put down the number of the month in which she was born, then to multiply it by 2, then to add 5, then to multiply it by 50, then to add her age, then to subtract 365, then to add 115, then tell her to tell you the amount she has left. The two figures at the right will tell you her age, and the remainder the month of her birth. For example the amount is 822; she is 22 years old and was born in the eighth month (August). Try it.

Anon
Marshall's Illustrated Almanac, 1908

If there be another chair in the room, do not offer a lady that from which you have just risen.

George S. Appleton
Etiquette for Gentlemen, 1848

Oh, will Heaven grant I may love and be loved someday.
Then I shall be engaged.

Sarah Elizabeth Jewett
In her diary, 1840

In making an evening call a man should appear about half-past eight, and remain an hour. Even if his visit is to the daughter, he should ask for her mother.

When a young man is paying a visit, and the older members of the family are in the room, he should, in leaving, bid them good-night first, and afterward say his farewell to the young girl on whom he has called. It is in bad taste for her to go any further than the parlor door with him.

X. C.
Practical Etiquette, 1899

Carriage Dress

There is much latitude for display permitted by the carriage dress. Rich materials, elegant wraps, costly furs, are all allowable here.

Coaching parties, too, have grown to be occasions for most gorgeous costuming. Every hue of the rainbow is to be seen as the lofty tally-ho rolls past.

Maud Cooke
Social Etiquette, 1896

Miss Tousey.

The Wearing of Ornaments

A young girl, and especially one of a light and airy style of beauty, should never wear gems. A simple flower in her hair or on her bosom is all that good taste will permit.

Allen and McGregor
The Ladies' Guide, 1902

Dinner-Dress

Young unmarried ladies may wear dresses of lighter materials and tints than married ones. But whatever color the dress may be, it is best to try its effect by gaslight and daylight both, since many a color which will look well in daylight may look extremely ugly in gaslight.

Richard A. Wells
Manners, Culture
and Dress, 1890

A True Measurement

However well a lady has appeared at a party, I would recommend to a young gentleman — before he makes up his mind to her domestic qualities — to observe her appearance at the breakfast table, when she expects to see only her own family.

An American Lady
The Ladies' Vase, 1847

WANTED A MATCHMAKER

When Cupid Calls

WITH A THOUGHT BLESS ME

xii   PREFACE.

written in this ma... ... spel wa...

...sters of this art, as CICERO's Let-
...ciently evince: nor are the Moderns
...ble of its excellencies. Some of the
...rench writers have built their fame upon
Epistolary correspondence: and the English
are at present so convinced of the advantages
attending this method of conveying their sentiments, that it seems to have triumphed over
almost every other species of composition: the
Historian has adopted it; we have the Greek
and Roman histories, as well as that of our
nation, admirably executed in letters. Almost
every thing didactive and perspective, is deli-
vered in this ... ...the Novelist finds it better
adapted ... ...of writing ...than any other mode
...mili... ...ect is without his fa-
seeme... ...the Traveller
veyin... ...od of con-

To... ...trade,
the fu... ...ship, the
food o... ...ainment
of the... ...we love or
esteem... ...n we are ca-
pable of... ...ext is, being able
to conve... ...by letter.

DIRECTIONS

FOR

WRITING LETTERS.

It was a just observation of the honest Qua-
ker, that, if a man think twice before he speak,
he'll speak twice better for it. With great
propriety the above may be applied to all sorts
of writing, particularly the Epistolary. In
letters from one relation to another, the different characters of the persons must be first considered: Thus a father in writing to a son will
use a gentle authority; a son to a father will
express a filial duty. And again, in friendship, the heart will dilate itself with an honest
freedom; it will applaud with sincerity, and
censure with modest reluctance. In letters
concerning trade, the subject matter will be
constantly kept in view, and the greatest per-
spicuity and brevity observed by the different
correspondents; and, in like manner, these

(12)

Anticipated
→ Bliss ←

You can hardly think of anything more joyous in life, than to live with her in some old castle, very far away from steamboats, and post-offices, and pick wild geraniums for her hair, and read poetry with her, under the shade of very dark ivy vines. And you would have such a charming boudoir in some corner of the old ruin, with a harp in it, and books bound in gilt, with cupids on the cover. And when the minister reads off marriage announcements in the church, you think how it will sound one of these days, to have your name, and hers, read from the pulpit;——and how prettily she will blush; and how poor little Dick, who you know loves her, but is afraid to say so, will squirm upon his bench.

Donald G. Mitchell
Reveries of a Bachelor, 1850

Do you LIKE ME?

Proposals

I seized Mary Rose's prayer-book, and turning over the pages till I came to matrimony, marked the passage, "Wilt thou have this man to be thy wedded husband?" with two emphatic dashes; and pointing significantly and confidently to myself, handed it to her with a bow. She took it!—she read it!—she smiled!!!

"Popping the Question"
Godey's Lady's Book, 1832

*I*t is probable that every lover, before he makes his passion known, exercises his fancy in the formation of some pretty or eloquent phrase for conveying the tremendous secret that masters his heart; but where one lover remembers his fine speech at the critical moment, perhaps a hundred will forget.

Daphne Dale
Our Manners and Social Customs, 1902

WILL YOU BE TRUE?

$\mathcal{I}$ was woefully disappointed when the mail came in last night bringing no letter from Mr. Boyce. It is not possible that he has not written. No, 'tis some rascally post-master—I wish they were all turned out or locked up in their own mailboxes.

Sarah Elizabeth Jewett
In her diary, July 11, 1841

$\mathcal{I}$t is said Queen Victoria "put the question" to Prince Albert by showing him Windsor and its beauties and the distant landscape, and then quietly saying, "All this may be yours."

Fannie Dickerson Chase
Good Form and Social Ethics, 1913

$\mathcal{O}$h! to feel I was, and am, loved by such an Angel as Albert was too great delight to describe! he is perfection; perfection in every way.

Queen Victoria
In her journal, October 15, 1839

A Written Proposal

I seal the letter, and carry it — a great weight — for the mail. It seems as if there could be no other letter that day; and as if all the coaches and horses, and cars, and boats were specially detailed to bear that single sheet. It is a great letter for me; my destiny lies in it.

Donald G. Mitchell
Reveries of a Bachelor, 1850

Postage Stamp Flirtation

Stamp placed upside down on the left-hand corner of the envelope signifies — I love you.

Same corner, crosswise — My heart is another's.

Same corner, straight up and down — Goodbye, sweetheart.

Upside down on the right-hand corner — Write no more.

In the center at top — Yes.

In the center at bottom — No.

On the right-hand corner at right angle — Do you love me.

On left-hand corner at right angle — I hate you.

Top corner at right — I wish your friendship.

Bottom corner at left — I ask your acquaintance.

On line with surname — Accept my love.

The same, upside down — I am engaged.

Anon
Reeves Pocket Companion, 1886

The Jolly Postman.

A Woman's Chance to Marry

¼ of 1 per cent., from 50 to 56 years of age.

⅜ of 1 per cent., from 45 to 50 years of age.

2½ per cent., from 40 to 45 years of age.

3¾ per cent., from 35 to 40 years of age.

15½ per cent., from 30 to 35 years of age.

18 per cent., from 25 to 30 years of age.

52 per cent., from 20 to 25 years of age.

14½ per cent., from 15 to 20 years of age.

Anon
Romance of the Zanigs, 1904

Who Should We Marry?

A man with very light flax-colored hair should not marry a woman with hair of the same color; nor should a man with deep colored red hair marry a woman with hair of the same deep color . . . for it will be bad for the children.

L. U. Reavis
Young Men and Young Women of America, 1871

Oracle des dames.
Qu'est-ce que l'amour?

Pour consulter l'oracle
il suffit de penser une lettre,
de tourner la roue et de lire
la réponse correspondante.

The Unmarried Man

We deplore the fact that because of the fearful extravagances of modern society many of our best people conclude that they cannot possibly afford to marry.

We are getting a fearful crop of old bachelors. They swarm around us. They go through life lop-sided. Half dressed, they sit round cold mornings, all a-shiver, sewing on buttons and darning socks . . . we do not pity them at all. May all their buttons be off to-morrow morning! Why do they not set up a plain home of their own and come into the ark two and two?

T. DeWitt Talmage
Around the Tea Table, 1874

Too Many French Bachelors

Recently published French statistics show that there are over two million men . . . who utterly fail to appreciate the beauties of matrimony. In other words, nearly one-fourth of the adult male population of France are bachelors, and propose to remain so. Such a frightful state of affairs could only exist in a population devoted entirely to pleasure and totally regardless of duty.

The Young Ladies Journal, 1886

The Kiss

You think back upon some time when in your games of forfeit, you gained a kiss from those lips; and it seems as if the kiss was hanging on you yet, and warming you all over. And then again, it seems so strange that your lips did really touch hers! You half question if it could have been actually so,—and you wonder if you could have dared;—and you wonder if you would have the courage to do the same thing again?—and you snap your fingers at the thought of it.

Donald G. Mitchell
Reveries of a Bachelor, 1850

What the Lips Tell

Well defined and developed lips, the outlines of which are rounded out, denote a tender-hearted, amiable and sympathetic disposition.

The lower lip, according to its fullness, freshness in appearance and width, indicates benevolence and liberality.

Well closed lips indicate discretion. If the upper lip is long in addition to being pressed down firmly upon the lower lip, it shows power of both mental and physical endurance. People with long, firm upper lips disregard the opinions of other people and are both dignified and proud.

When the corners of the mouth descend, a despondent disposition, prone to dwell upon the serious side of life, is indicated. When the corners turn up, however, in the form of a Cupid's bow, the possessor is of a bright, cheerful nature, always finding a silver lining to every cloud and seeing good in everything.

Anon
Romance of the Zanigs, 1904

Engaging Pastimes

Asking Papa

❧❧❧

Nelly?"

"Yes, sir—Nelly."

"What! Have you told all this to Nelly—that you love her?"

"I have sir."

"And she says——"

"That I must speak with you, sir."

"Bless my soul, but she's a good girl!"

And the old man wipes his eyes.

"Nell! Are you there?"

And she comes blushing, lingering and smiling through it all.

"And so you loved Will all the while?"

Nelly only stoops to drop a little kiss of pleading.

"Well Nelly, give me your hand—here Will, take it: she's a wild girl, be kind to her, Will?"

"God bless you, sir!"

Donald G. Mitchell
Dream Life, 1851

A Token of Love

One sees a young girl looking on her engagement ring as if she were reading her fate in some new chiromancy, and prays it shall be only joyous. How much is held in that little circlet, and how precious and how hallowed the engagement ring is to all lovers!

Harriet Prescott Spoffard
House and Hearth, 1891

The bridegroom is permitted to give jewelry, a bouquet, a fan, a locket, and an engagement ring, but he is not allowed to send dresses or other necessary articles, unless as in the olden time, a camel's hair shawl, now entirely out of fashion.

M.E.W. Sherwood
Correct Social Usage, 1903

To get the right size required is not one of the least interesting of the delicate mysteries of love. A not unusual method is to get a sister of the fair one to lend one of the lady's rings to enable the jeweler to select the proper size.

Nugent Robinson
Collier's Cyclopedia, 1883

The prevailing fashion in England is very pretty, and may be recommended to those in this country who can afford it. Engagement rings are set with stones so selected that the initial letters of the names of the gems shall in construction form the Christian or pet name of the lover.

James D. McCabe
The National Encyclopaedia, 1879

The bridegroom's present to the bride may take any form which his purse justifies. It may be a piece of jewelry; it may be a house and lot; it may be anything she longed for and will prize. She is giving herself, and is not supposed to supplement this extreme gift with any other.

Margaret E. Sangster
Good Manners for All Occasions, 1904

She Is Mine

You grow unusually amiable and kind; you shake hands with your office boy, as if he were your second cousin. You joke cheerfully with the stout washerwoman; and give her a shilling over-change, and insist upon her keeping it; and grow quite merry at the recollection of it. You tap your hackman on the shoulder very familiarly, and tell him he is a capital fellow; and don't allow him to whip his horses, except when driving to the post-office.

You think all the editorials in the morning papers are remarkably well-written—whether upon your side, or upon the other. You think the stock-market has a very cheerful look.

You give a pleasant twirl to your fingers, as you saunter along the street; and say—but not so loud as to be overheard—"She is mine—she is mine!"

Donald G. Mitchell
Dream Life, 1851

November 3, 19--.

*D*earest Albert:—

Your affectionate letter touched me deeply.
You asked me a very momentous question, to name
the day of our marriage. Dear Albert, it shall be as
you wish; your arguments are so convincing I can
only feel that you are right, and say yes to all you
propose. My mother also thinks that the 28th of
December would not be too soon, and that I can
make all my preparations within that time; there-
fore let it be the 28th. The period of our engagement seems very brief, indeed, but I have such
perfect trust in you, and we know each other so
thoroughly, that I need not postpone our marriage
with the idea of seeing more of you, and can look
forward to our passing a very happy
life together.

Goodbye, dearest Albert;
fondest love

From your own

Alice

The Social Letter-Writer, 1900

Fixing the Day

Any hour between half past ten in the morning and nine at night is perfectly fitting to celebrate, with a greater or less degree of conventional pomp and circumstance, the plighting of marriage vows. But a wedding of the extremest fashion is usually celebrated at high noon, or twelve o'clock precisely, in imitation of the English custom.

Emily Holt
Encyclopaedia of
Etiquette, 1901

It is the expected bride's prerogative to name the "happy day." Tastes are divided as to the most desirable months. May is shunned by those who are in the least superstitious, as it is deemed unlucky. . . . the same as Friday is considered an unlucky day and the 13th of the month an unlucky date. . . . still it is the apple-blossom month in the north and one can have an apple-blossom wedding, which is very sweet and suggestive, but who had not rather have a June wedding, with June roses, or an October wedding, with the leaves all red and golden?

Annie Randall White
Twentieth Century Etiquette, 1900

CUT-OUT SUPPLEMENT NEW YORK SUNDAY AMERICAN AND JOURNAL, SUNDAY, OCT. 18, 1903.

An October Bride

DIRECTIONS—Cut out following outside line... ...pretty clothes and bouquet, ...following outside line... ...over shoulders. For ...shoulder straps down ...tongue A through t... ...by inserting ...veil and fit on t... ...top of ...hand! For th... ...and put on t...

Copyright, 1903, by W. R. Hearst.

Best Wishes

Hints to the Bashful Lover
Always Hold Her embroidery Silks

Embroidery Silk

The Bride's Garden Hat

Selected by Ida Cleve Van Auken
Drawings by M. E. Musselman

CERTAINLY there has never been a time when the more picturesque types of hats were so graceful in line and form as this year. Not a stiff, unbending shape can be found, the touch of the artist and the skilful devices of the millinery designer have been combining to give a delightful expression of harmony in the color, materials and shape. For the warm days of summer a wide-brimmed shade hat, becomingly shading the face, is charming with a light and airy afternoon gown. Smaller hats often possess a more piquant grace and cannot be entirely ignored, as they sometimes seem to be more in keeping with the character of the gown worn, or better adapted to one's proportions of figure.

Designed by M. Maurice

Designed by M. Maurice

Designed by M. Maurice

The Bride's
➤ Trousseau ➤

One or two evening dresses might be desired, and if one is of black net or lace it will be very useful. An evening wrap would be necessary. A plain tailor-made cloth gown for travelling, shopping and street wear and another gown of handsome cloth for visiting, luncheons and receptions. A pretty dress for days at home may be of pale-gray cloth, crepe de Chine or cashmere, high in the neck.

A satin foulard or taffeta, a thin cloth dress—voile or a like light material—a short cloth skirt for morning wear with shirt-waists, are all quite important. The thin summer frocks must be decided upon for quality and quantity by the bride-elect herself.

The Bride's Rose Dress

Designs by Mary Anderson Warner: With Drawings by M. E. Musselman

ROSES in June are so unques-
tionably the bride's flowers
that it seems most fitting to have her
good-time dress trimmed with different varieties of these beautiful
flowers. On the right is pictured
a dainty frock of canary-
silk and chiffon, most
trimmed with tiny
and foliage.
The roses m
of ribbon, a
that can b
good res
marqui
founda
and i
r q

Dressing-jackets
of silk or flannel and
a lounging gown of
cashmere or silk may be
added, these to be worn
in one's bedroom, be it
understood, and not
elsewhere.

Lingerie should
be marked with the
bride's initials or
monogram. A pretty
idea is to write the
first name on the
material and
embroider over
this marking. . . .

Eight of each kind of undergarment would be a very moderate supply. This would include eight each of night-dresses, drawers, chemises, corset-covers, skirts, short white and flannel skirts and undershirts of silk or wool. Shoes, slippers, corsets, gloves, hats and an umbrella should be in the list, and as many dozen handkerchiefs and stockings as can be afforded. Two silk underskirts would be found useful.

The household linen should also be supplied by a bride's parents. Six sheets, six pillow and bolster cases, two pairs of pillow shams and four spreads should be allowed for each bed. An ornamental coverlet of colored silk or embroidered linen is a charming possession. Four dozen towels would be a moderate supply. Six tablecloths and four or six dozen napkins, large and small, would be needed, and one handsome tablecloth, with napkins to match, for dinner parties. A few embroidered centrepieces and a dozen or two dainty doilies are attractive additions.

W. H. Kistler
Weddings, 1905

Shopping List

Have now altogether	$51.40
Narrow black lace 4 yards	1.75
Silk lining	.87
Green velvet narrow	.75
1 bolt white satin ribbon	1.25
2 yds. swiss muslin	1.50
Blue sewing silk	1.20
Whalebones	.20
Cord	.06
4 spools green silk	.16
Waist lining for silk	.44
Hooks & Eyes	.05
2 doz. lace buttons for organdies	.16
Hoops	1.75
Corsets	5.00
2 prs. gloves	3.75
Shoes	7.25
3 belts	1.35
1 yd. green ribbon	.31
Pins	.06
Mama's dress trimming	1.20
poor child	.20

Sallie B. Pendleton Van Rensselaer
In her journal, May 2, 1864

The Settlement

The marriage settlement is an important point. No parent or guardian should allow his child or ward to marry without having a part of her fortune secured upon herself. It is quite advantageous to the husband as to herself, since, in case of unlooked-for loss or misfortune, there is a sure provision for his wife and children.

An allowance for the lady's dress and pocket money should always be made, and so administered that the wife will not have to ask for it in season and out of season, but receive it as promptly as if it were a dividend.

Preparations for the Day

If you live in a large city like New York, and are rich enough to afford it, you need give yourself little trouble about the details of any ceremony. You have only to engage Mr. Brown, or some similar undertaker of weddings, funerals, and other fashionable occasions, and everything will be ordered and directed in the most stylish manner, and at whatever cost you may require. All you have to say is "Mr. Brown, my daughter is to be married Tuesday week — Grace Church—two hundred dollars." "Mr. Brown, a little wedding party at my house on the 17th—about, say, two hundred people, and cost—well, six hundred dollars." It will be done; and if your visiting list is short of the requisite number, Mr. Brown will furnish you guests of the most unexceptionable style and deportment—dancing gentlemen, supper men, literary, artistic.

Robert de Valcourt
Illustrated Manners, 1865

Wedding Cards

About ten days or a fortnight before the day of the ceremony, cards are issued. These consist of the separate cards of the bride and bridegroom, and two cards of invitation, on one of which there are merely the name and situation of the church, with the date and time of the ceremony, and on the other the names of the parents, thus associated: "Mr. and Mrs. John Smith," and an invitation to the house conveyed by the words "at home," with the address of the paternal mansion, and the date and hour of the reception. All these cards are put into one envelope, and sent to the relatives and intimate friends of both parties.

Robert Tomes
The Bazar Book of Decorum, 1872

Who Should Be Asked to the Wedding

The parties who ought to be asked are the father and mother of the gentleman, the brothers and sisters (their wives and husbands also, if married), and indeed the immediate relations and favored friends of both parties. Old family friends on the bride's side should also receive invitations.

On this occasion the bridegroom has the privilege of asking any friends he may choose to the wedding; but no friend has a right to feel affronted at not being invited, since, were all the friends on either side assembled, the wedding breakfast would be an inconveniently crowded reception rather than an impressive ceremonial.

Nugent Robinson
Collier's Cyclopedia, 1883

May good health and
Good fortune speed you.

Choice Gifts

For the people who must depend on their purse for their gift, the following list may be of service: grape scissors; asparagus tongs; gravy spoons; plate warmers; oyster forks; lobster pickers; tiny sugar tongs for four o'clock tea sets; a cream and sugar cruet for tarts; plaques; single fruit plates; china ornament; Japanese cabinet for stationery; brass trays and bowls for fruits; rose balls for jewel cases; or any thing in the line of useful or ornamental fans; real lace sets; jabots and handkerchiefs of thread lace, are all useful and handsome.

No one need be ashamed to give a cookery book, a book of etiquette, selections of poetry and prose. A library edition of Shakespeare or an illustrated copy of some popular poem will be suitable bridal gifts for gentlemen to send. Quaint and curious things do not cost more than some commonplace ones, and they are much more desirable to possess. A gold thimble, pearl penknife, silver and gold card case, cameo ring, silver shawl and hair pins may be given by near friends. Choice perfumery in small bottles, which can be had in pairs in Russia leather cases, silver drinking cup and chain, pilgrim bottles and gypsy camp kettles, incense jars are all considered desirable.

M. L. Rayne
Gems of Deportment, 1881

Wedding Gifts on Display

*I*n opulent families each has sometimes given the young couple a silver dinner service and much silver besides, and the rooms of the bride's father's house look like a jeweller's shop when the presents are shown. All the magnificent ormolu ornaments for the chimney-piece, handsome clocks and lamps, fans in large quantities, spoons, forks by the hundred, and of late years the fine gilt ornaments, furniture, camel's-hair shawls, bracelets—all are piled up in most admired confusion. And when the invitations are out, then come in the outer world with their more hastily procured gifts; rare specimens of china, little paintings, ornaments for the person—all, all are in order.

M. E. W. Sherwood
Manners and Social Usage, 1884

Something New in Wedding Presents

We learn from a valued Kansas exchange which comes to us weekly that an important wedding took place there recently. This was not remarkable in itself, nor perhaps, were the wedding offerings, though they are worth passing mention. "Among the many beautiful and costly presents to the happy couple were a fine double-barrelled shotgun from the groom's father and an excellent shorthorn cow, a remembrance from the bride's mother. Jim was already possessed of a good pointer dog, so he is now well fixed for housekeeping."

It seems to us that these are a sufficiently radical departure from the conventional wedding presents to demand a moment's attention. What an oasis they are in the weary desert of duplicate silverware and diamond brooches! How refreshing it must have been to the guests, with visions of the usual thirteen pickle-casters and forty-eight individual salt-cellars, to step up to the parlor table and find a good centre-fire, hair-trigger shotgun!

The reader will not fail to note the closing sentence of the quotation we make from our Kansas friend. It is a pleasure to learn that the groom was already provided with a dog.

The idea that we are becoming conventional, that the stiffness of European formality is creeping among us, does not seem to hold water when investigated in the light of such occurrences as this Kansas wedding. The affair in no way resembled the late royal marriage in England. Europe may cling to the silver service and the jewelry, but free and untrammelled America will continue to mark out new paths in the way of wedding presents, if it takes all the firearms and livestock in the country.

New York Daily Tribune
September 7, 1889

Souvenirs & Celebrations

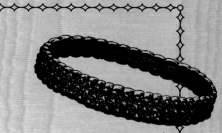

*T*he groom generally presents some *souvenir* of the occasion to each of the bridesmaids and ushers, fans, rings, bangles, and miniatures, prayer-books and lamps, and canes, scarf-pins, sleeve-buttons and spurs, are among the objects bestowed to remind the receivers of their opportune services. The bouquets of the maids and *boutonnières* of the ushers are the gift of the bride.

Abby B. Longstreet
Social Etiquette of New York, 1887

A tribute of Affection

Menu for a Bride's Luncheon

Hot Bisque of Clams, in cups

Lobster Patties   Olives   Vegetable Salad

Rolls

Fruit Sherbet   Macaroons

Coffee

W. H. Kistler
Weddings, 1905

The Bride's Farewell Luncheon

*I*t is always a gay occasion and one at which all the old superstitions dear to girlhood are invoked to foretell the future of each maiden present.

When the cake is cut to see who receives the ring, the silver dime, the tiny silver heart, the diminutive horseshoe, the little silver cross, the anchor or the thimble, each may determine her fortune from the trinket contained in her portion.

Good cheer and merry chatter are the order of the day, with toasts and kindly wishes for the bride-elect.

At this feast the bride presents her maids with the souvenirs, which should all be alike and be worn or carried at the wedding.

W. H. Histler
Weddings, 1905

The Bachelor's Farewell Dinner

Two or three evenings before his marriage, the bridegroom usually gives, at his club or at some hotel or restaurant, a dinner to his best man, ushers and sometimes a few other good friends.

A pretty conceit is to have a centrepiece of roses, and toward the close of the repast to send it to the bride-elect with a gallant or humorous message from each gentleman present. The best man proposes the health of the bride, and all present, standing, drink to this.

The guests find at their places scarf-pins or other souvenirs from their host, which must be worn at the wedding.

W. H. Kistler
Weddings, 1905

MARRIED LIFE

Now the rite is duly done,
Now the word is spoken,
And the spell has made us one
Which may ne'er be broken.

The
Bride
and
Groom

True Love

She is gentle;——keeping your love, as she has won it, by a thousand nameless and modest virtues, which radiate from her whole life and action. She steals upon your affections like a summer wind breathing softly over sleeping valleys. By a single soft word of appeal, she robs your vexation of its anger; and with a slight touch of that fair hand, and one pleading look of that earnest eye, she disarms your sternest pride.

You read over the marriage service,——you will take her hand, and slip the ring upon her finger; and repeat after the clergyman——'for richer——for poorer, for better——for worse.'

When you approach that day which is to make her yours, there are no flowers rare enough to make bouquets for her; diamonds are too dim for her to wear.

Donald G. Mitchell
Dream Life, 1851

Bridal Omens

However unlucky or undesirable tears may be on all other occasions, on one's wedding day it is best to shed a few, according to old tradition. They are sure to bring good luck.

♥ It is a very excellent thing to wear something borrowed upon the wedding day; it also brings plenty of good luck, though, so far as one's natural idea would go, both the above would be anything but "lucky."

♥ One of the most beautiful of all marriage customs is that of the bride, immediately after the ceremony, flinging her bouquet among her maiden friends. She who catches it is supposed to be the next bride.

♥ Of course the bride must cut the first piece of the bride's cake; just why no one exactly knows, but perhaps it is to signify that she is now a hostess and should serve her guests.

♥ The bride should also serve the first glass of wine, if it is used at all, at the wedding feast.

♥ There is a legendary or mythical prejudice against anyone handing the bride a knife for the purpose of cutting the bride's cake. If there has not been one set apart and tied with a ribbon, she avails herself of any knife lying near.

♥ In provincial England the cook pours hot water over the threshold after the bridal couple have gone in order to keep it warm for another bride.

♥ At a Hebrew wedding, man and wife sip from one cup of wine, symbolizing participation in the joys and pains of earthly life. The emptied goblet is placed on the floor and crushed into a thousand pieces by the bridegroom, who thus shows that he will put his foot on all evils that may enter the family circle.

♥ In leaving the church, the bride should make her exit through the same door as that by which she entered. It is unlucky to enter by one door before the ceremony and leave by another afterward.

♥ The bride should always be the first to call her husband by his name after the ceremony.

♥ While it may not be quite convenient after the wedding feast, the bride should lose or throw away all pins used in her costume. It is unlucky to retain them, and it will bring bad luck to the bridesmaids if they pick them up and keep them.

W. H. Kistler
Weddings, 1905

At the Dressing Table

It is doubtful if there is a bride that does not cherish every happy omen.

Among old superstitions, it is "unlucky" for a bride to look at herself in the glass after she is completely dressed; so the bride of to-day "for fun" puts on a glove or other trifle of attire after the last look has been taken in the mirror. Upon the arrival of her bridesmaids she gives to each "for luck" a garter which she herself has worn. Before the moment for departure, she is left entirely alone for a brief while, during which time blessing, not luck, is invoked.

Mrs. Burton Kingsland
Etiquette for All Occasions, 1901

The hair is dressed in front with small curls and a tuft of orange blossoms. The back hair is arranged in a waterfall, with a few light curls hanging over it. A tulle veil is thrown over the head and covers the face.

Sarah Josepha Hale
Godey's Lady's Book, 1865

She was simply a dear, sweet girl until she named her wedding-day, and became the pivot on which material things depend for adjustment and the centre of the family emotions. Even the younger children and the servants are eager to share in the common devotion, and from the tying of her shoe-string to the glitter of her costliest wedding gift, nothing is of any comparative interest in the household.

For months of preparation the needs and purposes of other members of the family are put into the background. Every item of wardrobe and household plenishing is of supreme value in their thoughts and in their conversation.

The tide of excitement grows stronger and deeper day by day until at last, be the household of what status it may, on the eve of the wedding, there is literally no other thing thought of but the event and its central white-robed figure.

"C"
Home Thoughts, 1901

$\mathcal{M}$amma came before and brought me a Nosegay of orange flowers. . . . I wore a white satin gown with a very deep flounce of Honiton lace, imitation of old. I wore my Turkish diamond necklace and earrings, and Albert's beautiful sapphire brooch.

Queen Victoria
In her journal, February 10, 1840

"The Bride"

The Bridal Gown & Veil

The traditional attire for a bride is a white satin gown of rich quality—or silk, if preferred—the skirt plain, with gracefully sweeping train. It is trimmed with lace and orange blossoms simply or elaborately, according to the taste or means of the wearer, and the veil of tulle or rich lace is held in place by a wreath or spray of orange blossoms. A wealthy bride is privileged to wear a tiara for the first time on her wedding day, it not being a jewel appropriate to girlhood. Diamond stars of graduated sizes, made detachable for wearing in other ways, is the favorite form of the diadem.

The bride sometimes wears her veil over her face as she goes up the aisle, but returning it is thrown back, showing her happy face to the world.

Mrs. Burton Kingsland
Etiquette for All Occasions, 1901

The bride wore a large diamond star, the gift of the bridegroom; pearl necklace, with diamond clasp and pendant, the gift of the bridegroom's sisters; bar pin of seven diamonds on the front of the corsage, the gift of the bridegroom's mother.

The bride wore white satin brocaded in silver, with full train and V-shaped corsage. The entire gown was veiled in old point de Venice, which was worn by her mother and grandmother on their wedding days. The veil of the same lace was held by orange blossoms and a diamond tiara. She held a silver prayer-book set with jewels.

The bride, a petite brunette, wore an exquisite gown of white faille française draped with duchesse lace and a long moiré antique train.

Dempsey & Carroll
Wedding Etiquette, 1889

She carried a bouquet composed of five bunches of roses, in one of which was hidden a ring, in accordance with a pretty superstition that the bridesmaid securing the bouquet with the ring will first of all become herself a bride.

The Bride's Bouquet

No prettier arrangement of flowers was ever made than in the form of a "shower bouquet" for the bride. The custom came from England, but America has adopted it most willing. The shower bouquet is defined in its name; it is literally a falling rain of roses.

These shower bouquets are almost equally ribbons and roses. The ribbons are cut in varying lengths and fastened together at one common centre. The fragrant buds and blossoms are knotted at intervals all along these ribbon lengths, and so tied on that the blooms of one ribbon overlie the silken spaces of another, making a massed yet loosely-falling abundance of perfumed floral beauty. The bride's hand is nearly concealed as she carries this bouquet. The trailing ribbons hidden beneath the flowers fall down to the hem of her bridal gown and she walks up to the chancel "a thing of beauty" to the beholders.

At the wedding reception the bride frequently cuts the flower-covered ribbons of her bouquet into bits, which she distributes to her attendants and friends as pretty souvenirs of the happy occasion.

Adelaide Gordon
Correct Social Usage, 1903

Red Roses
TRUE LOVE

Roses speak love
The whole world through,
That is why I send
Roses red to you.

No one I love.

How to Press Flowers

To preserve the delicate colours it is necessary that they should be dried at once. Place them on drying-paper and carefully arrange every flower.

Lay several sheets over and under, and put in a press or under a heavy weight. You will never regret the few shillings invested in a press. Twelve hours after pressing change the papers and press again. In a few days they will be ready to lay away.

Woman's Life, 1899

Mother and I went over the river to do some shopping, bought my *wedding dress*! It is plain Swiss muslin. I wanted white satin but could not have it so concluded to have it pass for beauty unadorned! After all I wish I could stand up in my every day frock sometimes without a fuss.

*Sarah Elizabeth Jewett
In her diary, July 15, 1841*

Forget me not

Summer may change to winter,
Flowers may fade and die,
But I shall ever love thee
While I can heave a sigh

Language of Flowers
Forget-me-not:
"Forget-me-not."

→ The ← Bridegroom

The groom at a wedding is always secondary in importance to the bride. He generally manages to make his bow, and he always succeeds in carrying off his blushing bride, which is probably all he came for.

Mrs. Burton Kingsland
Etiquette for All Occasions, 1901

What a Bridegroom May Pay For

Most bridegrooms would, from the fullness of their hearts, pay for everything connected with the coming event, but this would offend the delicacy of the bride and her friends. There is a law of etiquette concerning this, as all other matters.

He should not fail to send the wedding bouquet to the bride, on the morning of the ceremony. He also should, if his means permit, present the bride with some article of jewelry.

He should pay the clergyman's fee; bouquets to the brides-maids; scarf-pins, canes, sleeve buttons, or any other little remembrance which his ingenuity may suggest, to the groomsmen.

Annie Randall White
Twentieth Century Etiquette, 1900

The groom sends carriages to convey the ushers to and from the church and he provides not only the carriage in which he and his best man go to the church, but also the one in which he and his bride drive away after the ceremony.

Emily Holt
Encyclopaedia of Etiquette, 1901

What He May Wear

The present style of evening dress has been much abused, as so closely resembling that worn by waiters. The black tail-coat, waistcoat, and trousers, and white tie, present a sombre, not to say a gloomy appearance, and furnish no scope for variety from year to year, except in the shape and cut. A little brightness has been lately introduced in the shape of coloured silk socks and shoes. An attempt was made some few years since to effect a great transformation in evening dress, and to introduce a costume somewhat of the olden style—black velvet coat and small clothes; an embroidered waistcoat, also made of black velvet; scarlet or black silk stockings, and shoes ornamented with large silver buckles. This innovation did not meet with either universal acceptance or a hearty welcome.

Anon
Etiquette of Good Society, 1899

I F I were a
rain-drop
and you a leaf,
I would burst from
the cloud
above you,
And lie on your
breast
in a rapture of rest,
And love you—
love you—
love you!

Sweet Dreams

Only two Sundays more, dear Nelly, and one of them I hope to spend with you! I *hope*, but don't feel *sure*, of anything in this matter, except that I shall *be there at the* wedding.

I long for the happy day! No regret, or fear, or misgiving mingles with my joy, in view of our marriage; but, O Nelly! how much of my future happiness depends upon you—how much of yours upon me!

Dearest love, good-night. Dream of me! Dream that I fold you in my arms and kiss you again and again, as I say once more *good-night, sweet wife!*

Louis
A Manual of Letter Writing, 1857

I do not sleep well that night;—it is a tossing sleep; joy—sweet and holy joy comes to my dreams, and an angel is by me.

Donald G. Mitchell
Reveries of a Bachelor, 1850

*H*ow are you to-day, and have you slept well? I have rested very well, and feel very comfortable to-day. What weather! I believe, however, the rain will cease.

Send one word when you, my most loved bridegroom, will be ready. Thy ever-faithful, Victoria R.

Queen Victoria
In her note to Albert on their wedding morning,
February 10, 1840

RADIANT.

To GREET YOU ON YOUR WEDDING MORNING.

THE SWEETEST OF ALL BLESSINGS.
I WOULD CHOOSE
To BLESS YOU BOTH, IF BUT
THE CHOICE WERE MINE,
Life's HAPPY SUNLIGHT
MAY YOU NEVER LOSE
But TREAD IN
PATHWAYS WHERE IT'S
GLAD RAYS SHIN[E]

WEDDING MARCH. MENDELSSOHN

Willmer. ROTARY PHOTO. E

7549-G.

The Carriage to the Church

The happy *cortège* should proceed in the following order:

In the first carriage, the bride's mother and the parents of the bridegroom.

In the second and third carriages, bridesmaids.

Other carriages with the bride's friends.

In the last carriage, the bride and her father.

Nugent Robinson
Collier's Cyclopedia, 1883

When the day of the wedding has actually dawned each moment is full of happy import. If the vows are to be spoken at church, the bridal party, in their own carriages, or in those provided by the bride, drive to the bride's home and, without alighting, await her readiness to proceed with them to the church.

Adelaide Gordon
Correct Social Usage, 1903

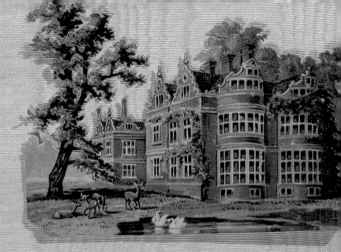

Occasionally the bridal coaches are distinguished by having wedding favors of white flowers on the head-stalls of the horses and in the servants' coats.

Mrs. Burton Kingsland
Etiquette for All Occasions, 1901

The bride's father is of necessity obliged to have carriages in readiness to meet guests at the railway station, to convey them to the church and afterwards to the reception, and again to the railroad station; and this arrangement need not be mentioned in the invitations.

Emily Holt
Encyclopaedia of Etiquette, 1901

Mindful of his duty to serve ably, her cavalier stands near the front wheel, but well outside it, leaving ample space for her descent between the front and rear wheels. Extending his right hand, the muscles of his arm stiffened to meet and support her weight, he takes her fingers with a firm grasp and lowers his elbow gradually as she comes down, while with his left hand he guards her gown from contact with the wheel.

Emily Holt
Encyclopaedia of Etiquette, 1901

The Ceremonial Procession

The Wedding Day

The day for your marriage comes; and you live as if you were in a dream. A flood of charity seems to radiate from all around you. For she has said it, and her mother has said it; and the kind old gentleman, her father, has said it too; and they have all welcomed you——won by her story——with a cordiality, that has made your cup full, to running over. Only one thought comes up to obscure your joy;——is it real? or if real, are you worthy to enjoy? Will you cherish and love always, as you have promised that angel who accepts your word, and rests her happiness on your faith? Are there not harsh qualities in your nature, which you fear may sometime make her regret that she gave herself to your love and charity? And those friends who watch over her, as the apple of their eye, can you always meet their tenderness and approval, for your guardianship of their treasure? Is it not a treasure that makes you fearful, as well as joyful?

Donald G. Mitchell
Reveries of a Bachelor, 1850

The Best → Man ←

He is the necessary ark of safety to this agitated groom. He accompanies him to church, he follows him to the altar, he sees to it that he has the ring in his pocket, he stands at his right hand, a little behind him, during the ceremony, he attends to all his small wants, holds his hat and afterwards pays the clergyman his fee. Then in a coupe all alone by himself the best man follows the young couple home, and assists the ushers to introduce friends to the bridal pair.

M.E.W. Sherwood
Correct Social Usage, 1903

At length the day fixed for their marriage arrived. Too proud to let Aubrey know that I had been his unsuccessful rival, I consented to officiate as groomsman on the occasion, but what mental torture did I suffer! I remember Edith's dress—ay, even to the little pearl clasps that fastened her snowy slipper, as if it had been only yesterday that I looked upon her bridal attire. The coronal of gems that bound her dark tresses, was my gift—the richly-jeweled bands that encircled her slender waist, and rounded arms, were my choice, but alas! the small gold chain that lay upon her bosom, was dearer to her than all my lavished treasures, for it held the picture of her idolized Frederick. They were married.

"Recollections of a Bachelor"
Ladies Companion Magazine, 1840

The Bride and the Bridal Party

Designs by Rowena Rice: With Drawings by Augusta Reimer

The Maid of Honor

The maid- or matron-of-honor stands nearest the bride during the ceremony; she holds the bride's bouquet or prayer book, also her glove — while the ring is being given. It is her duty to turn back the veil when the couple have been pronounced man and wife.

The maid-of-honor goes with the bride to her room to assist her in dressing for her wedding trip, and also casts the traditional slipper after the departing carriage.

She also assumes, during the absence of the bride, any little duties in the way of visiting elderly or invalid friends, and any kindnesses the bride may have been unable to express, through lack of time, are carried out by the maid-of-honor.

W. H. Kistler
Weddings, 1905

One lady is always appointed principal
bridesmaid, and has the bride in her charge; it is also her
duty to take care that the other bridesmaids have the wedding
favors in readiness. On the second bridesmaid devolves, with her
principal, the duty of sending out the cards; and on the third bridesmaid, in conjunction with the remaining beauties of her choir, the
onerous office of attending to certain ministrations and mysteries
connected with the wedding cake.

Nugent Robinson
Collier's Cyclopedia, 1883

Often when there are a number of bridesmaids, half the
number are attired in one colour, half in another. Sometimes
the choice rests with the chief "maid," but we think all should
consider and try to fall in with the wishes of the bride elect.

Anon
Etiquette of Good Society, 1899

"A-ling Ihear
the Bride Bells
ring"

And so thro' those dark gates across the wild
That no man knows. Indeed I love thee: come,
Lay thy sweet hands in mine and trust to me.

— Tennyson...

My bride,
My wife, my life
O we will
Walk this world
Yoked in all exercise
of noble end,

The Bridal Procession

The church was decorated with palms, ferns, and thousands of roses, intertwined among smilax and laurel, and were illumined by electric lights.

Midway in the main aisle was erected an arch, with gates of daisies, which were opened by nephews of the groom. The bridal procession was led by the surpliced choir, singing the bridal chorus from "Lohengrin." Then came the priest, followed by the ushers; then the brides-maids. . . . .

*Dempsey & Carroll
Wedding Etiquette, 1889*

The brides-maids' dresses were particularly pretty. They were made of some soft, light, cream-colored stuff, and completely covered with undulations of coffee-colored lace and creamy satin. Little man-of-war caps, also made of lace, had bunches of polyanthus in front.

*Mrs. M. L. Rayne
Gems of Deportment, 1881*

The bride in her white gown was preceded by two little girls in white frocks and large mob-caps, carrying baskets of syringa blossoms which they scattered on the bride's pathway. The baskets were inexpensive hats of yellow straw, bent and tied with pale-blue ribbons and slung on the arm. The wedding ring was placed in the heart of a calla lily, and was carried in by a three-year-old ring-bearer. When children carry the ring it is best to tie it with tiny white ribbon and pin it by a small loop to the cushion or flower, as little hands grow nervous and may drop it.

*W. H. Kistler
Weddings, 1905*

Last of all comes the bride, leaning on her father's arm. As she reaches the lowest step of the altar stair the bridegroom advances to meet her, takes her right hand, conducts her to the altar, and the clergyman then proceeds to make the pair one.

*M. E. W. Sherwood
Correct Social Usage, 1903*

The Marriage ❖ Ceremony ❖

The twain are made one as if by the touch of the enchanter's wand, and the command enjoined that they shall go forth as husband and wife, pledged to cherish, love and protect each other, and to multiply and replenish the earth.

L. U. Reavis
Young Men and Young Women of America, 1871

The Past belongs to God: The Present only is ours. And as short as it is, there is more in it, and of it, than we can well manage.

Donald G. Mitchell
Reveries of a Bachelor, 1850

A Wedding-day! It is a day of rejoicing as it should be; but it is no less a day of life-long merriment.

Charles Titcomb
In a letter to Ellen, September 18, 1857

The Hoop of Fidelity

Sentiments to engrave in a Wedding Ring

"Ad finem esto fidelis" — Be faithful to the end.

"With heart and hand at thy command."

"Endless as this shall be our bliss."

Mrs. M. L. Rayne
Gems of Deportment,
1881

The best man takes the ring and gives it to the bridegroom, who passes it to the bride, and she hands it to the clergyman, who gives it the bridegroom who then places it on the fourth finger of the bride's left hand. This completes the circle, typical of the ring itself of the perpetuity of the compact.

Mrs. Burton Kingsland
Weddings, 1905

On the way home from church, the bridegroom may put the engagement ring back on the bride's finger, to stand guard over its precious fellow. . . . Some husbands, who like to observe these pretty little fancies, present their wives of a year's standing with another ring, either chased or plain, to be worn on the wedding ring finger, and which is called the "Keeper." This, too, is supposed to stand guard over the wedding ring.

Annie Randall White
Twentieth Century Etiquette, 1900

In many parts of Great Britain it is still supposed that a marriage without a ring is not binding.

Woman's Life, 1899

Among all the rings which ladies wear no one has attached to it the dignity and honor of the wedding ring. . . . The ring is a symbol of eternity and constancy, placed on the left hand of the woman to denote her subjection, and on the ring finger because it is said to press a vein which communicates directly to the heart.

George D. Carroll
Wedding Etiquette, 1889

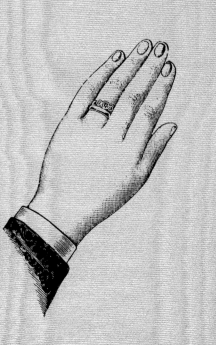

A reason exists for the choice of the third as the ring finger. All the other fingers can be extended fully alone while its companions are folded in, but one cannot extend the third finger alone. This peculiarity makes it a safer place for a ring, should it be placed on the finger which always has a little bodyguard of its fellows.

Woman's Life, 1899

The engagement ring remains on the third finger of the left hand until just before the marriage ceremony, when it should be transferred to the corresponding finger of the right hand, the wedding ring taking its place on the left hand.

W. H. Kistler
Weddings, 1905

RING CARD

Following the → Ceremony ←

The bride leaves the altar, taking the bridegroom's right arm. They pass down the aisle without looking to the right or to the left. It is considered very bad form to recognize acquaintances by bows and smiles while in the church.

Mrs. H. O. Ward
Sensible Etiquette, 1878

If favors are given they are distributed generally by the brides-maids, while the wedding party is still in the vestry. Ladies' favors are usually a spray of jessamine or myrtle with silver leaves and white satin ribbon; the gentleman's, a spray of oak leaves and acorns with silver and green leaves without ribbon. The brides-maids' favors are slightly more ornamental, and often have a spray of forget-me-nots.

Mrs. M. L. Rayne
Gems of Deportment, 1881

At a recent wedding a joyous peal of bells announced the arrival of the bride at the church door, and again the joy bells rang a merry peal as she left the church. It was indescribably suggestive of light hearts and bright hopes.

Mrs. Burton Kingsland
Etiquette for All Occasions, 1901

*A*mong the bright and pleasant variations to the solemn pomp of a church wedding which etiquette heartily approves, is the strewing of flowers in the path of the young couple as they go away from the altar. Little girls, costumed in white, with baskets of blossoms, rise up, like unsuspected fairies, while the clergyman is congratulating the bride, and slowly drop roses down the aisle to the carriage. Sometimes garlands of flowers, that have been somewhere hidden, are suddenly seen stretched across the aisle at brief intervals, by little maidens who stand on the seats at the ends of the pews, and lift their pretty arms high in air to swing their roses over the pathway of the bridal party.

Sometimes, instead of garlands, they toss rose-leaves in crimson, gold, and white from the same high positions, all over the outgoing procession.

Abby B. Longstreet
Social Etiquette of New York, 1887

The Mother of the Groom

The mother whose son is receiving the highest prize life can offer, be she ever so generous, feels a little bereft. She will not again possess her son as a member of her family, in just the fullness that has hitherto been hers. She is not jealous, yet she is wistful, wondering whether her boy will be understood and cared for and happy as he has been under her care.

The Mother of the Bride

As for the bride's mother, her feelings are strangely compounded by bitterness and sweetness. She cannot be altogether at ease in her mind. This dear child has been to her another self. When the carriage rolls away, and the wedding festivities are over, the bride's mother may be pardoned if she wanders away to Mary's old room, and, kneeling down by Mary's bed, pours out her soul in a flood of tears. The first evening after the wedding is a saddened one in the home the bride leaves.

When the Princess Victoria of England was married to the Crown Prince of Germany, as the ceremony was finished, she threw herself impulsively into her mother's arms. That touch of nature drew tears from eyes all around the globe. Most mothers weep when their daughters are wedded, and yet they are not weeping for sorrow. They are, as I heard a mother once say, "tearfully proud," for no mother is regretful when her daughter is a bride.

Margaret E. Sangster
Good Manners for All Occasions, 1904

MARRIAGE CERTIFICATE

A Warm
Reception

The Celebration

A brilliant marriage——at which you receive a very elegant welcome from your wife's spinster cousins,——and drink a great deal of champagne with her bachelor uncles. And as you take the dainty hand of your bride,——very magnificent under that bridal wreath, and with her face lit up by a brilliant glow,——your eye, and your soul, for the first time, grow full. And as your arm circles that elegant figure, and you draw her toward you, feeling that she is yours,——there is a bound at your heart, that makes you think your soul-life is now whole, and earnest. All your early dreams, and imaginations, come flowing on your thought, like bewildering music; and as you gaze upon her, it seems to you, that all that your heart prizes, is made good by marriage.

Donald G. Mitchell
Reveries of a Bachelor, 1850

A Formal Reception

The bridal party came up from Philadelphia in a steamboat, and were conveyed to the shore in a rowboat, whose sides were completely hidden by flowers, and whose oars were covered with roses, while the rowers were in costume. A wide hallway runs through the house, and the door at the back opens on to a stretch of green lawn that slopes down to the Delaware. A strip of crimson carpet was spread from this doorway over the green lawn to the landing-place on the river, and over this the bridal party walked.

Dempsey & Carroll
Wedding Etiquette, 1889

The wedded pair, after receiving the congratulations of the officiating minister and saluting each other, take their places at once beneath the floral bell or arch, where the friends crowd to receive them.

Mrs. M. L. Rayne
Gems of Deportment, 1881

A pretty wedding custom, and one nearly always followed, is that of grouping the bridesmaids in a semi-circle just beyond that point where the newly wedded couple stand to receive good wishes and congratulations. Every bridesmaid holds her bouquet in her gloved hands, and aids in forming a sort of glittering train to the important stars of the occasion.

Emily Holt
Encyclopaedia of Etiquette, 1901

Many Happy Returns.

The Wedding Day

I love, it is our wedding day:
And not a thrush in woodland bowers.

Bridal Party

How to Make a Wedding Bell

If a wedding bell is to be used, hang this in the arch. One can readily be constructed at home from three hoops of diminishing sizes, hung together with cord, the largest hoop at the bottom. Cover with green and line with white bunting, using a single perfect rose for a clapper. Hang by ropes of the green.

W. H. Kistler
Weddings, 1905

At the wedding supper a wedding-bell of ice cream and bride roses are served at the bride's table. Ices served from hats and baskets of spun sugar are a popular style for weddings.

W. H. Kistler
Weddings, 1905

The Wedding → Breakfast ←

When the breakfast is sent from a confectioner's, or is arranged in the house by a professed cook, the wedding-cake is richly ornamented with flowers, in sugar, and a knot of orange-flowers at the top. At each end of the table are tea and coffee. Soup is sometimes handed. Generally the viands are cold, consisting of poultry or game, lobster-salads, chicken or fish *à la Mayonnaise*, hams, tongues, potted-meats, prawns, and game-pies; raisins, savory jellies, sweets of every description—all cold. Ice is afterwards handed, and, before the healths are drunk, the wedding cake is cut by the nearest gentleman and handed round.

George W. Carleton
Habits of a Good Society, 1865

Toasts to the Wedded Pair

Love without deceit and matrimony without regret.

May love and reason be friends, and beauty and prudence marry.

May the sparks of love brighten into a flame.

May the bud of affection be ripened by the sunshine of sincerity.

May a virtuous offspring succeed to mutual and honorable love.

Nugent Robinson
Collier's Cyclopedia, 1883

The bridesmaids cut the cake into small pieces, which are not eaten until the health of the bride is proposed. This is usually done by the officiating clergyman.

Nugent Robinson
Collier's Cyclopedia, 1883

Heartiest Congratulations

An Evening → Feast ←

At an evening wedding the regulation wedding "breakfast" is replaced either by a dinner, supper, or a collation—that is, the distribution of light refreshments, of which the guests partake in the most informal manner. When a dinner is served the regulation order for a formal dinner is observed. For a supper, several small tables are generally used in preference to a single large one, and when the assemblage is large, the guests adjourn to the supper room in successive relays, according to the seating capacity of the room. Hence it is that a buffet repast is usually preferred. An excellent menu for a dinner is here given:

Clam Broth   Oyster Bouillon
          Canapes Lorenzo
    Terrapin   Lobster à la Newburg
Chicken Croquettes   Sweetbread Patties
          Sandwiches
          Galantine of Chicken
          Larded Game in Aspic
Chicken Salad   Mayonnaise of Salmon
    Asparagus Salad   Cheese Patties
    Pistachio Charlotte   Wine Jelly
          Strawberry Mousse
    Coffee   Cake   Bonbons

W. H. Kistler
Weddings, 1905

Should there be dancing at a wedding, it is proper for the bride to open the first quadrille with the best man, the groom dancing with the first bridesmaid. It is not, however, very customary for a bride to dance, or for dancing to occur at an evening wedding.

M. E. W. Sherwood
Manners and Social Usage, 1884

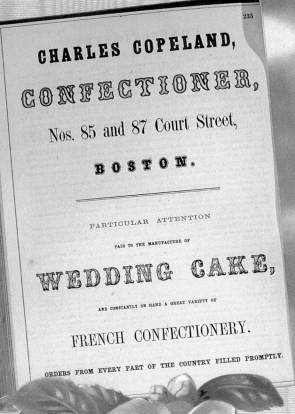

Cakes.

SUGGESTIONS IN REGARD TO CAKE MAKING.

Use none but the best materials, and all the ingredients should be properly prepared before commencing to mix any of them. Eggs beat up much lighter and sooner by being placed in a cold place some time before using them; a small pinch of soda sometimes has the same effect. Flour should always be sifted before using it. Cream of tartar or baking-powder should be thoroughly mixed with the flour; butter be placed where it will become moderately soft, but not melted in the least, or the cake will be sodden and heavy. Sugar should be rolled and sifted; spices ground or pounded; raisins or any other fruit looked over and prepared; currants, especially, should be nicely washed, picked, dried in a cloth, and then carefully examined, that no pieces of grit or stone may be left amongst them. They should then be laid on a dish before the fire to become thoroughly dry; as, if added damp to the other ingredients, cakes will be liable to be heavy.

Eggs should be well-beaten, the whites and yolks separately, the yolks to a thick cream, the whites until they are a stiff froth. Always stir the butter and sugar to a cream, then add the beaten yolks, then the milk, the flavoring, then the beaten whites, and lastly the flour. If fruit is to be used, measure and dredge with a little sifted flour, stir in gradually and thoroughly.

Pour all in well-buttered cake-p[…]
be taken that no cold ai[…]
cake is baking pro[…]
cold or too hot[…]

Cake is[…]
oven. T[…]
by throw[…]
takes fi[…]

The Wedding → Cake ←

*W*edding-Cake is a dark and rich fruit-cake. This time-honored dainty is an indispensable feature of the properly conducted wedding now as ever; the modern fashion being to have the cake cut into small wedges and packed in dainty white boxes, tied up with white ribbon, previous to the ceremony. The boxes are then put aside on the hall table in a convenient place, ready for distribution when the guests depart.

Each departing guest takes from the hall table as a souvenir of the wedding one of these boxes of wedding-cake, which should be fancifully piled up.

W. H. Kistler
Weddings, 1905

Recipe for a Wedding Cake

Four pounds of flour, three pounds of butter, three pounds of sugar, four pounds of currants, two pounds of raisins, twenty eggs, half a pint of brandy, or lemon brandy, one ounce of mace, three nutmegs. A little molasses makes it dark-colored. Half a pound of citron improves it. To be baked two hours and a half or three hours. An excellent receipt.

Sarah Josepha Hale
Godey's Lady's Book, 1865

Almond Icing for a Wedding Cake

Beat the whites of three eggs to a strong froth, pulp a pound of Jordan almonds very fine with rose water, mix them, with the eggs, lightly together; put in by degrees a pound of common loaf sugar in powder. When the cake is baked enough, take it out, and lay on the icing; then put it in to brown.

Anon
Inquire Within, 1895

The Bride's-Cake

Bride's-Cake is a frosted white cake. It is, of course, a specially prepared confection, and is not to be confounded with any one of the various kinds of cake served in the ordinary course of the festivities. The old custom of placing a gold ring and a silver thimble in the cake is still occasionally observed, but when this is done the cake is cut and distributed by the bride herself. The guest to whom the ring falls is supposed to be destined to speedy marriage, while she who secures the silver thimble is positively foreordained to spinsterhood.

*W. H. Kistler
Weddings, 1905*

The Queen's Bride-Cake

We have been favoured with a sight of it, and it surpasses in design, as well as in dimensions, any bride-cake ever seen. It is more than nine feet in circumference, by 16 inches deep. Two pedestals rise from the plateau of the cake, the upper one supporting another plateau, whereon stands Britannia gazing upon the royal pair, who are in the act of pledging their vows. At their feet are two turtle doves, emblems of purity and innocence, and a dog representing faithful attachment; a little lower down, Cupid is seen writing in his tablets with his stylus the date, "February 10, 1840." On the same level with Cupid are black pedestals raised at equal distances flanking the royal group; on these pedestals are other Cupids, with the emblems of England, Ireland, and Scotland, in their hands, and supporting large medallions upon fantastic shields, with the initials V. A.

*The London Times,
February 1840*

The Wedding Guests

Wedding Dress for Men

At an evening wedding, full evening dress is the only costume possible. For a morning wedding, a black cutaway coat with waistcoat to match and gray trousers is always a proper costume. Gray gloves, patent leather or dull dongola shoes, white linen and a broadly-folded silk or satin tie, are the proper additions to either of these two costumes.

Wedding Dress for Women

The most elaborate afternoon reception costume is invariably worn to a church or house wedding held in the morning or the afternoon. Bonnets are not put off at a reception or a breakfast; gloves are laid aside only while one is in the act of eating.

At an evening wedding feminine guests wear elaborate décolleté toilettes if they choose, or very elaborate high-throated, long-sleeved reception toilettes without hats or bonnets.

Emily Holt
Encyclopaedia of Etiquette, 1901

Costumes and Customs

It is not considered lucky or appropriate to wear black at a wedding. In England the ladies of the bride's family who are in mourning wear deep cardinal red to the wedding.

M. E. W. Sherwood
Correct Social Usage, 1906

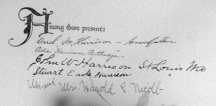

As the happy pair drive off, a shower of *satin slippers* and rice follows them. If one slipper alights on the top of the carriage, luck is assured to them forever.

Two white shoes at least are thrown, one by the chief bridesmaid, the other by the best man.

Mrs. M. L. Rayne
Gems of Deportment,
1881

The
pretty custom originated
in France. An old woman seeing
Louis XIII passing from church where he
had just been married, took off her shoe,
and flinging it at his coach, cried out: "'Tis
all I have, your majesty, but may the
blessings of God go with it."

W. H. Kistler
Weddings, 1905

GENUINE PHOTOS
of
NIAGARA FALLS
FOR YOUR ALBUM

W. D. KING

Souvenir

A VERY
YOUNG COUPLE

ALL eyes were
on me when
I boarded
the steamer.

YOU CAN
PUT YOUR ... IN MY

Forever
More

ing us up to the Station in
the train and a hush ... before
... for ... were white with dust
...hed London at ten o'clock at the
...tion and took a Hansom ...
...hrough the lighted streets ablaze
...wing shops. We reached the Hotel
... on the Strand and although
... had been reserved and prepared
... not resist the witchery of the
... so taxied up to the Criterion
... for a late supper and a new
...ople as they came in from
...tre a gay scene with good
...hen to bed. July 15th we
... early for our first day of ...

Alone at
❧ Last ☙

You enter your name upon the hotel books as "Clarence————
and Lady"; and come back to look at it,——wondering if any body
else has noticed,——and thinking that it looks remarkably well.
You cannot help thinking that every third man you meet in the hall, wishes
he possessed your wife;——nor do you think it very sinful in him, to wish it.
You fear it is placing temptation in the way of covetous men, to put her little
gaiters outside the chamber door, at night.

You wonder if the people in the omnibus know, that you are just
married; and if the driver knows, that the shilling you hand to him, is for
"self and wife?" You wonder if anybody was ever so happy before, or ever
will be so happy again?

Donald G. Mitchell
Dream Life, 1851

The Departure

Off for the Honeymoon

ARE WE DOWNHEARTED

down the stairs and through the hall, to the door, where he delivers her as a precious charge to her husband, who hands her quickly into the carriage, springs in after her, waves his hand to the party who appear crowding at the window, half smiles at the throng about the door, then, amidst a shower of old slippers—missiles of good-luck sent flying after the happy pair—gives the word, and they are off, and started on the long-hoped-for voyage!

Nugent Robinson
Collier's Cyclopedia, 1883

The young bride, divested of her bridal attire, and quietly costumed for the journey, now bids farewell to her brides-maids and lady friends. A few tears spring to her gentle eyes as she takes a last look at the home she is now leaving. The servants venture to crowd about her with their humble but heart-felt congratulations; finally, she falls weeping on her mother's bosom. A short cough is heard, as of some one summoning up resolution to hide emo-tion. It is her father. He dares not trust his voice; but holds out his hand, gives her an affectionate kiss, and then leads her, half turning back,

In England etiquette requires that the bride and groom should depart in state, with many wedding-favors on the horses' heads, and huge white bouquets on the breasts of coachman and footman.

It is in England, also, etiquette to drive with four horses to the place where the honey-moon is to be spent; but in America the drive is generally to the nearest railway-station.

M.E.W. Sherwood
Manners and Social Usage, 1884

A favorite dress for travelling is heliotrope cashmere, with bonnet to match. For a dark bride nothing is more becoming than dark blue made with white vest and sailor collar. Gray cashmere with steel passementerie has also been much in vogue. A light gray mohair, trimmed with lace of the same color, was also much admired.

Harper's Bazar, 1885

The Wedding → Tour ←

*A*fter looking about our rooms for a little while, I went and changed my gown, and then came back to his small sitting room where dearest Albert was sitting and playing; he had put on his windsor coat; he took me on his knee, and kissed me and was so dear and kind.

Queen Victoria
In her journal, February 10, 1840

An American Adventure

Windsor Castle
Oct. 22, 1847

*H*ere, we were to meet face to face *"Her Gracious Majesty The Queen of Great Britain"* and we had nobody to back us. We were alone. I took off my hat—and the lady sitting furthest from us began to bow. This was *Victoria*—she bowed several times, smiling, and looked back to us after she had passed. Whew! we are short of breath, we have been within a few feet of a living *Queen*, we have *seen her*, and she has *seen us*. "Long live the Queen."

George Endicott
In his journal

ONE MILE TO VANCOUVER

The honey-moon in our busy land is usually only a fortnight in the sky, and some few bridal pairs prefer to spend it at the quiet country house of a friend, as is the English fashion. But others make a hurried trip to Niagara, or to the Thousand Islands, or go to Europe, as the case may be. It is extraordinary that none stay at home; in beginning a new life all agree that a change of place is the first requisite.

M. E. W. Sherwood
Manners and Social Usage, 1884

I must not forget to mention the interesting and not over-youthful couple we met on the train from Toronto to Kingston—the groom took advantage of the slowness and frequent stopping of the train to pick posies for his bride, while she, in tender affection leaned her head upon his shoulder. They occupied the room next to us at the Hotel Frontenac, and ate at our table. They did not appear to have energy enough to stir from the hotel, but must have gotten as far as Montreal, for we met them there, coming home from church on Sunday.

Mrs. Alexander McMillan Welch
In her Wedding Book, 1896

Milestone near Vancouver brings us closer.

A Reception for the New Couple

*I*t is very common for the bride's parents to give the young couple a reception upon their return; this is followed by one given them by the parents of the groom. At these receptions, if she wishes, she can wear her wedding-dress but the veil and flowers are worn no more.

Annie Randall White
Twentieth Century Etiquette, 1900

*H*ERE in fortune's fairy boat
Is a cargo, rich and rare;
Blisses! Kisses! Health and Wealth!
Yours shall be the lion's share.

On Saturday afternoon, Dec. 19, 1896, Mama and I held a reception from four to seven. This reception was given to me by my parents as part of my marriage festivities. It was too late in the season for me to have it after my return from my wedding trip, in June, so we waited until we moved into our 71st Street home. . . . It gave our guests an opportunity to call upon us after the wedding. My maid-of-honor, ribbon girls, flower girls, and bridesmaids received with me. They wore the same gowns that they wore at my wedding. . . . Mama and I wore our wedding gowns. Mac also wore his wedding suit, and stayed near me to help receive our guests. Papa and Bashford were present all the afternoon. All our ushers came to the tea. . . . Bernstein and four men played the piano delightfully during the reception.

They were in the music room behind palms, furnished by Dards. Dards decorated the chandeliers beautifully with holly, and Johnston draped the mirrors and side lights with smilax, also filled the vases with flowers from our green house. Margadant served an elaborate supper providing service waiters. The day was a beautiful one, and the whole reception was most successful.

Mrs. Alexander McMillan Welch
In her Wedding Book, 1896

Mrs. Isaac M. Dyckman and Mrs. Alexander McMillan Welch gave a reception, Saturday, from 4 to 7, at 15 East 71st Street, New York City.

The Yonkers Statesman Newspaper,
December 20, 1896

At Home

*A*nd after marriage, the weeks are even shorter than before: you wonder why on earth all the single men in the world, do not rush tumultuously to the Altar.

Married men, on the contrary, you regard as fellow-voyagers.

You blush a little, at first telling your butcher what "your wife" would like; you bargain with the grocer for sugars and teas, and wonder if he *knows* that you are a married man? You practise your new way of talk upon your office boy;—you tell him that "your wife" expects you home to dinner; and are astonished that he does not stare to hear you say it.

Your home, when it is entered, is just what it should be:—quiet, small,—with everything she wishes, and nothing more than she wishes. The sun strikes it in the happiest possible way:—the piano is the sweetest-toned in the world;—the library is stocked to a charm;—and that blessed wife is there,—adorning, and giving life to it all. You grow twain of heart, and of purpose. Smiles seem made for marriage; and you wonder how you ever wore them before.

Donald G. Mitchell
Dream Life, 1851

*A*nd if your hearts are bound together by love; if both are yielding and true; if both cultivate the spirit of meekness, forbearance, and kindness, you will be blessed in your home and in the journey of life.

Matthew Hale Smith
Counsels to Young Men, 1850

*H*e called me names of tenderness, I have never yet heard used to me before—was bliss beyond belief! Oh! this was the happiest day of my life!

Queen Victoria
In her journal, February 10, 1840

Acknowledgments

This book was born out of some twenty years of collecting rare courtesy and etiquette manuals. To all those who joined my search and tucked away special finds for me, I am profoundly grateful.

For permission to use previously unpublished diaries and love letters, thanks to the Rare Book Department of the New York Public Library and to the New-York Historical Society. Thanks also to Martin Dibner and Paris Hill Press for permission to reproduce quotations from his book, *Portrait of Paris Hill.* My thanks to John Saddy (Jefferson Stereoptics, London, Ontario) for enriching my collection of wedding memorabilia throughout the years.

I am most grateful to Ken Lombardo who provided early inspiration in the creation of this book. Thanks also to Maggie Higgins, who carries a guiding light, and to Regina Ryan, my agent, whose counsel and tenacity proved invaluable.

To Monica Stevenson, a wonderful photographer who cheerfully brought my compositions to light and life, and to Kevin Amer for his darkroom expertise, heartfelt thanks. A fond thank you to Gloria Neumann for her generous and creative assistance during photography. And for her skill and untiring willingness to help with the manuscript, many thanks to Sarah Buckland.

I owe a great debt to my colleagues Jean Hoffman and Jana Starr (Jean Hoffman/Jana Starr Antiques, New York); Gerry Tandy (Gerry Tandy Antiques, Peekskill, New York); Barbara Muccio (Interesting Old Things, New York); Christine Pfeifer (White Mischief, Weehawken, New Jersey); Inger Kynaston (Inger of Sweden, New York); Judy Porter (Zuber & Cie, New York); and Hans Maarshalk and John Crowell (Roses Only, New York), who have all unfailingly and generously contributed to the pages of this book.

A most joyful happenstance of this book was having as my ever-enthusiastic editor Nancy Grubb, whose ideas sparkle throughout these chapters. Patricia Fabricant's disciplined design brought a welcomed order to my chaos. My deepest gratitude goes to them and to everyone else at Abbeville Press who worked to make this book such a delight.

Lasting appreciation also goes to Carolyn Barr, Barbara Bridendolf Ortbal, Ben Burns, Suzy and Ricky Carrick, Elizabeth and David Constable, Bernice Chardiet, Carl Friberg, Zena Intzekostas, William Kase, Donald MacDonald, Annick and Mark Obadia, Allan Temko, and Carmen Wyllie. This little first book is lucky to have so many friends. My sincerest thanks to one and all.

Sources for Victorian Bridal Gowns and Accessories

Originals

The Antiquarian
305 East LaSalle Street
South Bend, Indiana 46617
(219) 234-5941
Provides searches for specific
Victoriana.

Beverly Birks
1215 Fifth Avenue
New York, New York 10028
(212) 722-3263
By appointment only.
Haute-couture wedding gowns.

Christie's South Kensington
85 Old Brompton Road
London, England SW6 5LD
71-581-7611
The Textiles Department sometimes
includes Victorian wedding dresses
in their auctions.

Cocoa
7 Queens Circus
Montpelier, Cheltenham
Gloucestershire, England GL 50 IRX
42-233-5880
Antique tiaras for rent and for sale.

Deborah's Attic
719 South Limestone Street
Springfield, Ohio 45505
(513) 322-8842
Antique whites, including petticoats,
camisoles, and dresses.

Elaine Wilmarth Design Resources
5715 Sir Galahad Road
Glenn Dale, Maryland 20769
(301) 464-1567
Lacy Victorian accessories, plus
shawls, fans, and headpieces.

Ellen Johnson
2406 Wilshire Boulevard
Santa Monica, California 90403
(213) 829-5181
Antique whites, plus custom-made
"corset dresses."

Framm, Ltd.
2667 Main Street
Santa Monica, California 90405
(213) 392-3911
Custom-designed gowns made from
antique lace.

Gerry Tandy Antiques
1012 Park Street
Peekskill, New York 10566
(914) 737-1845
Satin bed-cap headdresses, unique
floral arrangements. She will acces-
sorize wedding parties, churches, and
receptions in the Victorian style.

Golyester
7957 Melrose Avenue
Los Angeles, California 90046
(213) 655-3393
Turn-of-the-century wedding dresses
and rare wax headpieces.

Interesting Old Things
315 East Eighty-sixth Street
New York, New York 10028
(212) 831-6498
By appointment only. Victorian
accessories for the bride.

Jean Hoffman/Jana Starr Antiques
236 East 80th Street
New York, New York 10028
(212) 535-6930
Hundreds of antique brides' and
bridesmaids' dresses, petticoats,
linens, shawls, and exquisite lace.

Katy Kane
34 West Ferry Street
New Hope, Pennsylvania 18938
(215) 862-5873
Wedding gowns in all shades of
white, dating as early as 1890.

Lacis
2982 Adeline Street
Berkeley, California 94703
(510) 843-7178
Lacy clothing and accessories. Will
also restore vintage pieces.

Linda White Antique Clothing
100 Main Street (Route 140)
Upton, Massachusetts 01568
(508) 529-4439
Lacy, white special-occasion dresses.

Lisa's Place
132 Thompson Street
New York, New York 10012
(212) 477-6027
Vintage wedding and evening gowns.

Lost Eras
1511 West Howard Street
Chicago, Illinois 60626
(312) 764-7400
Victorian accessories to style a
wedding.

Lunn Antiques
86 New Kings Road
Parsons Green
London, England SW6 4LU
71-736-4638
Antique veils, Edwardian tea dresses,
lace dresses.

Madame & Co.
117 Yesler Way
Seattle, Washington 98104
(206) 621-1728
Museum-quality and finely restored
Victorian gowns.

Natara's Collection
1396 Yonge Street
Toronto, Ontario
Canada M4T 1T7
(416) 928-7406
Antique veils, turn-of-the-century tea
dresses.

Opal White
131 Thompson Street
New York, New York 10012
(212) 677-8215
By appointment only.
Antique and vintage wedding dresses.

Out of the Past
9012 Third Avenue
Brooklyn, New York 11209
(718) 748-1490
Tea dresses, wedding gowns, *pointe-
de-gaze*-trimmed handkerchiefs.

Pahaka
19 Fox Hill
Upper Saddle River, New Jersey
07458
(201) 327-1464
By appointment only.
Long dresses dating from 1900.

Paris 1900
2703 Main Street
Santa Monica, California 90405
(213) 396-0405
By appointment only.
Turn-of-the-century dresses and custom-made rose-garland veils.

Portobello Market
Portobello Road
London, England W11
A Saturdays-only antique market. Bits
and pieces for a Victorian wedding.

Robinson Antiques
1236 Yonge Street
Toronto, Ontario
Canada M4T 1W3
(416) 921-4858
Antique-lace bodices, panels, and
bridal trains.

Somewhere in Time
103 Newcastle Drive
Lafayette, Louisiana 70503
(318) 235-1081
Victorian and Edwardian white petticoats and dresses. Custom-made
work also available.

Sweet Material Things
P.O. Box 689
Wallkill, New York 12589
(914) 895-2519
Brochure available.
Wedding gowns, matching head-
pieces, parasols, and accessories, plus
custom-designed dresses.

Virginia Antiques
98 Portland Road
London, England W11 4L2
71-727-9908
Antique veils, cut-velvet dresses, and
shawls.

White Mischief
752 Boulevard East
Weehawken, New Jersey 07087
(201) 601-9209
By appointment only.
Antique lace and linens, vintage
bridal clothing.

Yesterday's Threads
564 Main Street
Branford, Connecticut 06405
(203) 481-6452
Late Victorian and Edwardian tea
dresses.

Reproductions

Clare Wilson
Hobbits
Court Mead Road
Cuckfield
East Sussex, England RH17 5LP
44-441-3556
Historically accurate wedding gowns,
medieval to Edwardian.

Diane Harby
Tatters
74 Fulham Road
London, England SW3 6HH
71-584-1532
Custom-designed dresses enhanced
with old lace.

Diane Venengas
8704 Sunset Boulevard
Los Angeles, California 90069
(213) 659-6272
Antique lace and beadwork incorpo-
rated into traditional designs.

Holy Cross Stitch
6421 Locust Lane
Eldersburg, Maryland 21784
(410) 795-7455
Victorian and Edwardian dresses in
natural fibers only.

Monica Hicky
Bridal Salon, Saks Fifth Avenue
New York, New York 10022
(212) 753-4000
Designs for brides' and bridesmaids'
dresses in pure silks and French laces.

20th Century Frocks
Theydon Gallery, Loughton Lane
Theydon Bois
Essex, England CM161 JY
99-281-3770
Late-Victorian custom-designed
dresses.

Westminster Lace
1501 Fourth Avenue
Seattle, Washington 98101
(206) 622-4476
Victorian wedding gowns repro-
duced to fit today's sizes.
Branches in: Arlington, Virginia;
Bridgewater, New Jersey; Brea,
California; Burlington,
Massachusetts; Costa Mesa,
California; Dallas, Texas; Denver,
Colorado; Hackensack, New Jersey;
Los Angeles, California; Manhasset,
New York; McLean, Virginia;
Minneapolis, Minnesota; North
Bethesda, Maryland; Oak Brook,
Illinois; Palm Beach Gardens,
Florida; Palo Alto, California; Saint
Louis, Missouri; San Diego,
California; San Francisco, California;
Santa Clara, California; Sherman
Oaks, California; Stamford,
Connecticut; Walnut Creek,
California.

Institutions with Victorian Wedding Gowns and Accessories

Woodruff-Fontaine House
680 Adams Avenue
Memphis, Tennessee 38105
(901) 526-1469
Nineteenth-century weddings gowns on exhibit year-round; displays changed according to the season.

The Heritage Wedding Gown Collection
Amherst Museum
Colony Park
3755 Tonawanda Creek Road
East Amherst, New York 14051
(716) 689-1440
Nineteenth-century wedding dresses on rotating exhibit throughout the year, fashion shows, and rentals of a selected number of turn-of-the-century gowns.

The following institutions periodically exhibit their collections of Victorian wedding dresses—often in June. Check in advance to find out what is on view.

The Arizona Costume Institute
The Phoenix Art Museum
1625 North Central Avenue
Phoenix, Arizona 85004
(602) 257-1222

Chicago Historical Society
Clark Street at North Avenue
Chicago, Illinois 60614
(312) 642-4600

Costumes and Textiles Department
The Brooklyn Museum
200 Eastern Parkway
Brooklyn, New York 11238
(718) 638-5000

Detroit Historical Museum
5401 Woodward Avenue
Detroit, Michigan 48202
(313) 833-1805

Center for Costumes and Textiles at the Los Angeles County Museum of Art

5905 Wilshire Boulevard
Los Angeles, California 90036
(213) 857-6081

The Dugald Costume Museum
Box 38
Dugald, Manitoba
Canada R0E 0K0
(204) 853-2166

Elizabeth Sage Historic Costume Collection
AMID
Indiana University
Wylie Hall
Bloomington, Indiana 47405
(812) 855-5497

The Goldey Paley Design Center at the Philadelphia College of Textiles and Science
4200 Henry Avenue
Philadelphia, Pennsylvania 19144
(215) 951-2860

Indianapolis Museum of Art
1200 West Thirty-eighth Street
Indianapolis, Indiana 46208
(317) 923-1331

Margaret Melville Blackwell
History Museum
1208 Route 25A
Stony Brook, New York 11790
(516) 751-0066

The Costume Institute
The Metropolitan Museum of Art
Fifth Avenue at Eighty-second Street
New York, New York 10028
(212) 879-5500

Collections Department
Minnesota Historical Society
160 John Ireland Boulevard
Saint Paul, Minnesota 55101
(612) 296-6126

Missouri Historical Society
Jefferson Memorial Building
Forest Park
Saint Louis, Missouri 63112
(314) 361-1424

Museum of Art
Rhode Island School of Design
224 Benefit Street
Providence, Rhode Island 02903
(401) 454-6500

Costume Collection
Museum of the City of New York
Fifth Avenue at 103rd Street
New York, New York 10029
(212) 534-1672

The Oakland Museum
1000 Oak Street
Oakland, California 94607
(510) 834-2413

Museum of Costume and Textiles
51 Castle Gate
Nottingham
Nottinghamshire, England NG1
GAF
60-248-3504

The Museum of Fine Arts
465 Huntington Avenue
Boston, Massachusetts 02115
(617) 267-9300

The National Museum of Fashion
Fashion Institute of Technology
Seventh Avenue at Twenty-seventh
Street
New York, New York 10001
(212) 760-7708

Division of Costume, 4202
The National Museum of American
History
Smithsonian Institution
Constitution Avenue, N.W.
Washington, D.C. 20560
(202) 357-3185

Philadelphia Museum of Art
Twenty-sixth Street and Benjamin
Franklin Parkway
Philadelphia, Pennsylvania 19101
(215) 763-8100

San Antonio Museum Association
Box 2601
3801 Broadway
San Antonio, Texas 78299
(512) 829-7262

State Historical Society of Wisconsin
30 North Carroll Street
Madison, Wisconsin 53703
(608) 264-6555

Alan Suddon
Toronto
Ontario, Canada
(416) 924-6179
This private collector will show his
collection of wedding dresses, dating
from 1800, to serious textile students.

Valentine Museum
1015 East Clay
Richmond, Virginia 23219
(804) 649-0711

Textile Department
Victoria and Albert Museum
South Kensington
London, England SW7 2RL
71-938-8500

Wadsworth Atheneum
600 Main Street
Hartford, Connecticut 06103
(203) 278-2670

Western Reserve Historical Society
10825 East Boulevard
Cleveland, Ohio 44106
(216) 721-5722

Historic Costume and Textile
Collection
University of Washington
Seattle, Washington 98195
(206) 543-2100

First edition

Library of Congress Cataloging-in-Publication Data

Wedded bliss : a Victorian bride's handbook / [compiled by] Molly Dolan
Blayney.
p.   cm.
ISBN 1-55859-332-2
1. Wedding etiquette. 2. Courtship. I. Blayney, Molly Dolan.
BJ2051.W37 1992
395' .22—dc20

91-43680
CIP

*Go forth, little book! Wherever young hearts are bounding,
wherever Hope has reared a temple, be thou found. Be thou the
medium through which the lover woos his lady, a sweet remem-
brancer of other days, a cheering index to the Future. Go forth, my
little book! and blessings attend thee.*

Mrs. J. Thayer
The Golden Present, 1848